To all of my weird and wonderful family,
I love you all very much. x

First published in Great Britain 2020 by Red Shed, part of Farshore
This edition published for Scottish Book Trust in 2021 by Dean
An imprint of HarperCollins*Publishers*
1 London Bridge Street, London SE1 9GF
www.farshore.co.uk

HarperCollins*Publishers*
1st Floor, Watermarque Building, Ringsend Road
Dublin 4, Ireland

Text and illustrations copyright © Sophy Henn 2020
Sophy Henn has asserted her moral rights.

ISBN 978 0 0085 2194 3
Printed in the UK by Pureprint a CarbonNeutral® company
001

Consultancy by Paul Lawston.

A CIP catalogue record for this title is available from the British Library.

ALL KINDS OF
FAMILIES

Sophy Henn

All kinds of families come together in all kinds of ways.

Each one is very special . . .

. . . but no two are quite the same.

It's the same for animal families too.

**Here is a family where
Mummy looks after the babies.**

Orang-utan mummies look after their young
longer than any other animal parent,
and they do it on their own.

They love their babies very, very much.

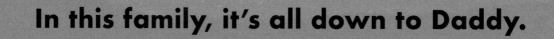

In this family, it's all down to Daddy.

Emu daddies have to work ever so hard to look
after their eggs, and they raise their chicks
until they are two years old.

And here is a family with a mummy and a daddy.

These clownfish parents are very, very busy keeping their underwater home clean and tidy for all their eggs.

Mummies can lay up to 1,000 eggs in one go!

Some families are big and busy,
so the older brothers and sisters
help look after the little ones.

Long-tailed tits live in large groups
of up to 20 birds who all look out
for one another. In the winter, everyone
snuggles together to keep warm.

Other families are so enormous that everyone helps to look after the babies.

In elephant families, one older
lady elephant is in charge. She shares
her knowledge with the younger family
members, so everyone keeps safe and well.

Sometimes grandparents
look after the youngsters.

Orca whales live for a very long time,
long enough to become grandparents.
Grandmothers often look after the young
while their mothers search for food.

There are also families with two mummies.

Sometimes female albatrosses
pair up and raise chicks together.

The two mummies stay together forever and ever.

Little ones who find themselves
without a family can be adopted.

This family has two daddies.
Every so often, two male cheetahs will
adopt a lost cub and raise them as their own.

And sometimes family can mean
friends and community.

Meerkats live in big groups of up to 50. Everyone has
a job – either gathering food, keeping watch or babysitting.
They all work together, so the group is safe and fed.

Yes, there are so many kinds of families, but they all have one thing that's the same . . .

love.

Now you've met their families, let's find out a little more about each animal.

Albatrosses in this book are called Laysan. There are lots of different types of albatross, such as the wandering albatross, which has the largest wingspan in the world – up to 3.5 metres.

Cheetahs are the fastest land animals in the world and can run as fast as a car on the motorway – 112 kilometres per hour! Unlike other big cats, cheetahs cannot roar, though they can purr.

Clownfish live in the coral reefs in the seas around Australia and South Asia. They help sea anemones by keeping them clean, and anemones help clownfish by protecting them.

Elephants are the largest land animals, and the biggest is the male African elephant. African elephants also have the biggest ears. They are the same shape as the continent of Africa.

Emus are the second-largest birds in the world, and they live in Australia. They have two sets of eyelids: one just for blinking and the other to keep dust out!

Long-tailed tits make their nests from grass, pine needles, lichen and cobwebs, which they thread together using only their beaks! They line the nests with feathers to keep the eggs and chicks snug.

Orang-utans are our very close relatives, and their name means 'person of the forest' in Malay. Both their hands and feet can grip, which makes them really good at moving through trees. They even sleep high up in big, leafy nests.

Orcas are the largest members of the dolphin family, with males growing up to 10 metres long! When they sleep, they only rest one side of their brain, while the other side stays awake to help them breathe.

Meerkats live in big groups called 'mobs'. They use their tails to help them stand up on their back legs, so they can warm their tummies in the sun after a long, chilly desert night.